WINTER SPORT: POEMS

WINTER SPORT: POEMS

Priscila Uppal

Mansfield Press

Library and Archives Canada Cataloguing in Publication

Uppal, Priscila
        Winter sport : poems / Priscila Uppal.

ISBN 978-1-894469-49-4

        1. Winter sport--Poetry. I. Title.

PS8591.P62W56 2010   C811'.54   C2010-905912-3

The publication of Winter Sport: Poems has been generously supported by
the Canada Council for the Arts and the Ontario Arts Council.

Design: Denis De Klerck
Cover Photo: iStockphoto
Author Photo: Jeff Kirk

Mansfield Press Inc.
25 Mansfield Avenue, Toronto, Ontario, Canada M6J 2A9
Publisher: Denis De Klerck
www.mansfieldpress.net

for those who risk everything
on talent

&

for the longest skating rink
in the world

Table of Contents

Dreaming Other People's Dreams   11

Winter Sport: Poems

Dreaming Other People's Dreams

While most people consider the worlds of sport and art as occupying radically different arenas – artists creating in their studios, athletes working out at the gym – athletes remind me very much of artists, and poets in particular. We dedicate ourselves to our disciplines regardless of whether or not we will receive financial rewards or compensation for our time or efforts. We strive continually to improve and refine our skills; we are obsessed with form, restrictions, rules, and finding ways of working imaginatively within constraints; we test and experiment with our bodies and minds to redefine and over-come barriers and limits. We are masters of pain management – the ability to manage pain, or to use pain as a transforming, rather than debilitating, force. We are fed by passion and the desire to be the medium that will create something beautiful, ethereal, magical, if only for a fleeting moment. Sport, like art, is about potential and possibility, dreaming and doing what it takes to shape that dream into reality. We hit limits, of course. But in sport and art, people test those limits all the time. When they test the limits, they encourage others to find ways to shat-ter those limitations. Sometimes it's the next generation that figures it out, but the trailblazers, even those who failed to achieve their goals, needed to press up against those boundar-ies before the boundaries could be broken down. It's an arena for those who ignore the naysayers, for those with stubborn souls and strong hearts, with a true desire for excellence and freedom. In both worlds exist dreamers, visionaries, rebels, perfectionists, experimenters, explorers, joy-seekers, geniuses, benevolent greats.

I have loved sports and the arts my entire life, and have been working actively over the last several years to create op-portunities for more dialogue and interaction between the two worlds, undertaking a number of projects, including editing the *The Exile Book of Canadian Sports Stories*, a unique anthology of sport fiction. I also acted as primary organizer (with poet and elite triathlete Dr. Suzanne Zelazo) of a three-day symposium at York University held in November 2009, entitled *Bodyworks: Intersections of Sport, Art, and Culture*, which brought together elite athletes, professional artists, researchers, academics, activists, students, and more, and included lectures, panels, literary readings, film screenings, and two art exhibitions featuring artwork by and about athletes. But my absolute favourite has been to act as Canadian Athletes Now Fund's poet-in-residence during the 2010 Vancouver Olympic and Paralympic Games – a position I designed, and which gave me not only the best gig at the games that I could imagine, but also the best poetry gig ever! My job: to engage poetically with winter sports; the games, the athletes, the fans, and the stories that captured the world's imagination. The poems in this book grew out of that experience.

Sport poetry? some asked, with amusement and skepticism. But is the genre really an oxymoron? Critic Ronald J. Meyers claims that the classical Greek poet Homer, in describing the funeral games in the epic *The Iliad* book XXIII, undertaken to give recognition to the hero (most of which survive into the present world of sport), was "the world's first sports writer." And here in Canada, each one of us carries a piece of hockey literature in our pockets, at all times. How Canadian is that? Don't remember? Take out your wallet, the blue bill, turn to its backside, and squint your eyes at the text just beside the skaters. In English and French, you will find the first line of the most famous Canadian short story of all time: Roch Carrier's "The Hockey Sweater," practically a Canadian anthem, a tragicomic parable of Anglophone and Francophone relations involving a little French-Canadian boy whose mother orders him a new #9 Rocket Richard Montréal Canadiens sweatshirt, but receives a Toronto Maple Leafs one from mail-order Eaton's instead. Even the parish priest punishes him for such blasphemous hockey attire.

And some of our most prominent and respected Canadian poets have written sport poems or utilized sport as metaphor in their verse: Margaret Avison, George Bowering, Anne Carson, Steven Heighton, Michael Holmes, Jim Johnstone, Irving Layton, Randall Maggs, David McGimpsey, Don McKay, David O'Meara, Al Purdy, Karen Solie, to name only a few. I also know many writers who play sport: some run to clear their heads (which is worth studying for societal benefits); some train in martial arts; some box; some ski; some swim; some play volleyball; some snowboard; many play hockey and softball.

Fine, you might relent. Sports poetry is legitimate. But a poet at the Olympics? Well, did you know arts competitions used to be included as part of the modern Olympic Games from 1912 to 1948? Medals were awarded for works of art inspired by sport, divided into five categories: architecture, literature, music, painting, and sculpture. Two people have actually won Olympic medals in both the sports and arts competitions: American Walter Winans, marksman and sculptor, and Hungarian Alfréd Hajós, swimmer and architect. Arts competitions were eliminated in 1954 because it was deemed artists were professionals, while Olympic athletes were amateurs. Now that this professional-amateur distinction, in both worlds, is much more blurred, why shouldn't we reconsider mounting the artistic competitions? Why is there such an overall dearth of high-quality art inspired by sport? Why does the art world consider sport a "minor" topic, unworthy of serious consideration? And why do so few sports enthusiasts find their passions reflected in contemporary art?

CBC, *The Globe and Mail*, and other media outlets (as well as other poets) have asked me my opinion on the inclusion of Shane Koyczan's spoken word poetry as part of the Olympics Opening Ceremonies. The fact that the inclusion of poetry in an arts spectacle – and I should add here that Koyczan's poem was not about sport – has caused such a stir of controversy and discussion is in itself an indication that something is seriously wrong. Why shouldn't poetry have a place among the music, dance, visual art, and architecture included in the Opening Ceremonies? For those who love poetry and the arts, and want to see them occupy a significant position in public life, which includes arenas like the Olympics, where the arts are intended to occupy a primary place (see the original Olympic mandate), this is a step in the right direction.

One of the problems, I think, that causes friction between artists and athletes is that artists can't claim to be ranked 1st or 2nd or even 115th in the world at what they do, and so criteria for judging, accepting, and celebrating are elusive, fluid, more dependant on critical voices, changing tastes and commercial acceptance than in the sports world where status is, mostly, determined by achievement and objective criteria agreed upon by sports organizations. I know this is also why I am drawn to the athletic sphere. Artists and athletes both love the competitive arena, but in sport, you can't fake it. You can either score that goal, land that triple axel, get to the finish line faster than your opponents – or you can't. My partner, poet and critic Christopher Doda, once made a group of Olympians, who were shrugging as they discussed their current 2nd, 5th, and 6th-place world rankings, laugh as he interjected, "I'd give my eye teeth to be ranked 10th in the world as a poet!"

And yet, fame in sport is elusive too. The person with the most talent, the most experience, the best technical skills, the consistent history of not breaking under pressure is still not guaranteed a win (or even a finish in a competition or race). We believe in an exchange of reward for effort, but fate sometimes has other ideas. And those in sport, as well as those who pursue excellence in the arts, are acutely aware that in any competition the majority lose. To win is the anomaly. The best-laid plans make the gods laugh.

At different times during my childhood and teenage years I played recreational and competitive basketball, volleyball, softball, tennis, hockey, and track. I played to escape my troubled home, to learn skills, to explore my body, make new friends, spend time with my brother, encounter other schools and cities, vent my anger, express my creativity, and get new clothes (we were poor and uniforms were provided). Now I still engage in sport, to stay healthy, to learn more about body science and innovation, to support athletes and teams, to raise money for charity, to force myself out of the house, to test my fears, to surrender to mystery, magic, tragedy, victory, and dreams, and to expand my artistic capabilities. In the last decade, I have taken lessons in fencing, figure skating, springboard diving, swimming mechanics, and running. And I now understand sport as a sister art to my work as a creative writer, and I firmly believe that sports practice and artistic practice should be discussed and researched together more often. I've learned a great deal about my artistic practice from sport practice: about clean aesthetic lines, gracefulness, trusting instincts, symmetry, compression of intricate movements, risk-taking, formal innovation, momentum, stamina, discipline, teamwork, offensive and defensive argument strategies, bravery, pain management, probabilities, humility. For instance, the compressed intricate movements of diving have taught me much about poetry; the steady discipline of running about novel writing; the quick swordplay of fencing about essay writing; and the performativity of figure skating about playwriting.

At York University, in creative writing classes, I tell my students to think of me as a coach – someone whose job is to push them, to make them sweat and suffer for the sake of their craft; someone they will hate on certain days and admire and thank on others. Students who have played competitive sports are usually much more willing to put in the hours of discipline needed to complete pieces of work. They don't expect it to be easy, and are less likely to shy away from struggle and the pain of the process. They know that, most likely, if they keep at it, they will see results. And even if they don't, the pain will have taught them something about themselves, or about the subject of writing that they didn't know before. Students who have played sport know what it's like to finish second, or third, or last. There's always somebody better than you, who possesses a different set of skills, a different fan base. Even successful athletes and artists are not necessarily going to survive in record books, canons, or halls of fame. One's lasting fame is frequently based on randomness, serendipity, historical factors, and plain chance. One must surrender to such justice.

Sport theorist Michael Novak, in "The Natural Religion," writes: "[S]ports flow outward into action from a deep natural impulse that is radically religious: an impulse for freedom, respect for ritual limits, a zest for symbolic meaning and a longing for perfection." Sounds like a description of poetry to me. A tight system of reference changes as the rules and players of a game change, much the way poets create elaborate metaphorical landscapes and poetics for their historical time and nation, and the experimental verse of one generation becomes the suffocating clichés to be surpassed by the next, just as athletes strive to break records and invent new skills and signature moves.

I think poets generally fall into two main categories: the celebratory poet (the poet of odes, the singer of praise), and the elegiac poet (the lamenter, the critic). Most of my work tends to fall on the elegiac side of the spectrum. The Olympics was my opportunity to explore the celebratory side of my poetic imagination, in the most genuine way I can imagine. I love the games, and sport, and especially the athletes and what they are able to accomplish with talent, will, determination, and a little luck. My aim as the Canadian Athletes Now poet-in-residence was to create poems that would bring the worlds of sport and art together in inventive, surprising, even amusing ways. Sports are rife with the drama of life, with full and rich metaphorical and symbolic possibilities, and with some of the coolest vocabulary around (snowboarding alone offers a myriad of linguistic delight that is playful, ecstatic, even erotic). Language links fans to sport, just as it links readers to poetry. I imagine these poems as verbal and metaphysical acrobatics existing harmoniously alongside their physical counterparts.

For instance, haiku emerged as a preferred form for this interplay. The Games' opening weekend coincided with Valentine's

Day, and the thought came to me that I would produce poems short enough to fit on postcards that I could hand out to the athletes as valentines. Most often, the form these poems took was the haiku. Several I ended up labelling "Love Haiku." While at first glance it might seem strange to write haiku about sport, the correspondences between the two are apt: 1) haiku tend to focus on images of nature: sports have their distinct seasons (winter, summer) and landscapes (lakes, ponds, hills, countryside); 2) haiku and sport are known for precision and clarity; 3) both can be meditative, awe-inspiring experiences of beauty; 4) the brevity of haiku mimics some sports competitions (which can be won or lost in less than the time it takes to read a haiku): 5) the strict syllable count in haiku mimics the strict numbers-based analyses of sport; 6) haiku engages in mental leaps, spiritual acrobatics: sport engages in physical leaps, transcendent bodily form; 7) both can be adapted to contemporary needs. I also thought the form would be one the athletes and the general public would have encountered in school, and therefore, while the pairing of sport with poetry might at first seem disorienting or baffling, people, young and old, would recognize the subject matter and hopefully also the poetic form in a non-threatening, appealing way. Reducing each sport down to an essence in seventeen syllables was challenging, but poetically inspiring. I found I couldn't stop. Some athletes told me they wanted to see the poems on T-shirts.

And, like the athletes, to accomplish my poetic feats, publishing two poems per day (posted on the Canadian Athletes Now and *Literary Review of Canada* websites, as well as additional media), I had to train, and then I had to prove my mettle through public performance. By training, I mean that I studied the rules, histories, judging criteria and terminology of all Olympic, Paralympic, and Arctic Games sports with the goal of writing a poem about each sport category: alpine skiing, biathlon, bobsleigh, cross-country skiing, curling, figure skating, freestyle skiing, ice hockey, sledge hockey, luge, Nordic combined, short track speed skating, skeleton, ski jumping, snowboarding, long track speed skating, Dene games, and arctic sports (for more on Paralympic and Arctic Games sports, see the essays at the end of this book). I read up on various Canadian athletes. I jotted down notes on the types of poems I might write – haiku, love poems, odes – and also the potential approaches I might employ: writing from the point of view of a piece of equipment, "if I could trade bodies" scenarios, new creative definitions for existing sport terms. I also had to live and breathe the Olympic, Paralympic, and Arctic Games experience, from pre-games buildup to last closing ceremonies, 24/7, attending events, speaking with athletes and their families, following the successes and tragedies of the day with genuine sympathy, compassion, admiration, and love.

And every day I put myself out there: online, in print, on radio and television, and in person, my poetic output on display for fans of poetry and sport alike. And nearly every evening, as part of gold medal celebrations at the CANFund Athlete House in the Shaw TV tower, as Sprott Asset Management LP in conjuction with the Sprott Foundation donated $100,000 to the fund for each gold medal won by Canadian athletes, I read a poem dedicated to the winning sport as part of the cheque presentation and champagne toast. Even though, at first, some of the athletes and their families were a little amused, even confused, by the sight of a young woman, braids in her hair, wearing a Team Canada Hockey jersey with the word "Poet" stitched on the back, scribbling away in her notebook, they turned out to be one of the most welcoming, supportive, and attentive poetry audiences I have ever encountered. They gave me their undivided attention during readings and asked for signed copies of poems. What at first was a novelty was soon a positive habit: "What's the poem tonight, Poet?" many of the athletes asked upon entering the house. Some even chanted, "Poet! Poet!" Over 120 athletes signed my jersey.

Over the six weeks that I spent attending the events and writing poems, I heard from friends and colleagues following my poetic postings and journalistic dispatches who were also swept up by games fever. One told me she lost her voice jumping up and down in her living room when freestyle skier Alexandre Bilodeau won the first Olympic gold medal on Canadian soil. (I'm not sure what was a more moving tribute to Valentine's Day – Canada finally winning that elusive gold or witnessing the bond of fraternal love between Alexandre and his brother Frederic, who is afflicted with cerebral palsy. The explosion of joy on Frederic's face as Alexandre crossed the finish line, arm pumping in the air, all teeth in his porkpie hat, renewed my long-standing query as to why there are few great love poems written for siblings.) Others asked about the atmosphere among athletes in sliding sports (luge, skeleton, bobsleigh) following the tragic death of Georgian luger Nodar Kumaritashvili. Others urged me to write a poem for brave figure skater, bronze-medallist Joannie Rochette, whose mother passed away during the games. Many expressed delight at the men's and women's hockey poems punning on the players' names. And following the men's gold medal win, a friend sent me a link to an overhead video of Vancouver's Cambie Bridge – all is quiet urban landscape and then you can literally hear the city rise with a roar as Sidney Crosby scores the overtime winning goal. A woman from Belgium I met at Paralympic cross-country skiing, who had never attended an event before, was off her seat, yelling, "Come on! Come on Canada!" as Brian McKeever passed his brother guide to take on the icy turns and pole his way to a smashing third gold-medal victory after suffering heartbreak from not being able to race in the Olympics. The games brought to life Olympic freestyle skier Ryan Blais' favourite quotation: "Adversity causes some to break, others to break records."

In sport and in art, dreams are admitted, openly, to the public. The athlete and artist are vulnerable, and no amount of training and talent and determination can completely guarantee the outcome. The race, a medal, a prize, a bestseller, is simply a visual or quantitative representation of the dream to succeed against the odds – to have one's dream undergo metamorphosis and step out of heart, mind, and body, and exist resplendently in front of all. Readers and spectators are invited to participate in the dream world of another person. It's emotional. It's scary. It's magical. When the dream is crushed by a fall or error or by another's dream, it's devastating.

I spent six weeks dreaming other people's dreams, my sleep filled with athletes and medals and glory and heartbreak. Talking to the athletes, writing poems for them and about sport, I was privileged to enter the space of the elite athlete and to invite the elite athlete and readers into my dream world as well. What is writing fiction and poetry if not giving verbal expression to dreams? And as so many of our summer Olympic hopefuls have expressed interest in this project, I'm committed to resuming my poet-in-residence position in 2012 in London and to publish the companion volume to this collection, *Summer Sport: Poems.*

On a much larger note, I would like to see the worlds of sport and art meet more, and on more creative terms. We are facing not only a physical health crisis in North America, and elsewhere in the world, but a creative crisis as well. We ought to embrace the dreams of athletes and artists and encourage people to live more physically and creatively active lives, not just to be healthier and smarter, but to experience the vibrant collective cultural exchange of these facets of our lives. May these three games also encourage our policy-makers and funding organizations to recognize the importance of sport and art for all – and to make the opportunities available equitable to all, including our women (who won more medals in the Olympics and Paralympics than the men), our aboriginal youth, and those with disabilities. The major organizing bodies of the Olympics, Commonwealth, and PanAm Games ought to adopt the Arctic Games' practice of inviting competing teams to bring artistic teams as part of their contingents, whose works comprise the bulk of the cultural component of the games (for more on this, see "The Arctic Games Experience" essay at the back of this book). By donating my royalties to the CANFund I wish to draw the public's attention to the fact that the world of sport is currently deficient in supporting our athletes: the vast majority are not able to afford the costs of competing at an elite level in their sport, even after winning Olympic medals.

In addition, I sincerely hope that this collection of poetry will make a contribution to Canadian literature, the teaching of reading and writing, and also to sport in Canada. Canadian institutions should consider teaching more sport literature and writing as a viable way to engage students, especially those not necessarily versed in literary history and theory, as an entry point into the world of art, which also ought to be open and accessible to all. Over the last year, I have started designing and mounting "Creative Writing Workshops for Athletes" and "Sports-writing Workshops," for youth and adults, hobbyists and elite athletes. Encouraging writing about sport is an exciting way to engage young men and women in the arts of poetry and literary prose and to break down stereotypes in the process. Training in writing offers elite athletes a practical and creative outlet to communicate their specialized knowledge – for blogs, websites, and journalistic dispatches while they are actively competing, as well as for future coaching and commentating when they retire from professional competitions.

Artists and athletes possess the same fundamental values and personalities. Both are passionate and focused, willing to risk and sacrifice almost everything in their lives to test their talents against others, the world, and ultimately the self. Dear reader, I invite you to camel spin, faceoff, corkscrew, nose slide, and slalom on and off these pages. Try on other people's dreams for size. Sometimes we need to dream other people's dreams in order to reimagine our own.

Winter Sport: Poems

Winter Olympics Parade

Albania aerials to Algeria
Algeria axel jumps to Andorra
Andorra Alley-Oops to Argentina
Argentina Air to Fakies to Armenia
Armenia assists Australia
Australia Andrechts to Austria
Austria alpine skis to Azerbaijan
Azerbaijan axis jumps to Belarus
Belarus bonks Belgium
Belgium bobsleighs to Bermuda
Bermuda brooms to Bosnia and Herzegovina
Bosnia and Herzegovina backside handplants to Brazil
Brazil bonspiels to Bulgaria
Bulgaria backscratches to Cayman Islands
Cayman Islands camel spins to Chile
Chile crossovers to China
China corner guards Chinese Taipei
Chinese Taipei crail airs to Colombia
Colombia curls to Croatia
Croatia critical grabs Cyprus
Cyprus corkscrews to Czech Republic
Czech Republic cross-country skis to Denmark
Denmark downhills to Estonia
Estonia eggplants to Ethiopia
Ethiopia Elgeurials to Finland
Finland four-point lands in France
France faces off with Georgia
Georgia gatekeeps Germany
Germany Gundersens to Ghana
Ghana glide waxes to Great Britain
Great Britain goofyfoots to Greece
Greece Super-Gs to Hong Kong
Hong Kong hurries hard to Hungary
Hungary herringbones to Iceland
Iceland ice skates to India

India Indy Airs to Iran
Iran ices the puck to Ireland
Ireland ironcrosses to Israel
Israel interval starts with Italy
Italy ice sledges to Jamaica
Jamaica Japan Airs to Japan
Japan J-tears to Kazakhstan
Kazakhstan K-points to Kyrgyzstan
Kyrgyzstan Kreisels to Latvia
Latvia lutz jumps to Lebanon
Lebanon lifts Liechtenstein
Liechtenstein luges to Lithuania
Lithuania lip tricks to Macedonia
Macedonia Mosquito Airs to Mexico
Mexico McTwists to Moldova
Moldova mono-skis to Monaco
Monaco mirror skates Mongolia
Mongolia mute grabs Montenegro
Montenegro Michalchucks to Morocco
Morocco moguls to Nepal
Nepal Narrows to Netherlands
Netherlands nosehits New Zealand
New Zealand Nollies to North Korea
North Korea Nordic Combines to Norway
Norway 900 Airs to Pakistan
Pakistan pushstarts Peru
Peru platterlifts Poland
Poland Pop Tarts to Portugal
Portugal pick-skates to Romania
Romania relays to Russia
Russia Rocket Airs to San Marino
San Marino Salchows to Senegal
Senegal skis classic technique to Serbia
Serbia ski jumps to Slovakia
Slovakia slaloms to Slovenia
Slovenia speedskates to South Africa
South Africa splits the house to South Korea

South Korea skeletons to Spain
Spain scramble legs to Sweden
Sweden sprints to Switzerland
Switzerland snowboard-crosses to Tajikistan
Tajikistan twizzles to Turkey
Turkey team sprints to Ukraine
Ukraine U-turns to the United States
United States upright spins to Uzbekistan
Uzbekistan Zudnicks to Canada
And Canada...

The Torch

Elemental, this world hike from Olympia
to the North Pole to the west coast of Vancouver.
45,000 kilometres and 106 days in Canada alone.

Just think of the multiplication of feet,
the metamorphosis of sunglasses to scarves,
the stunned looks of animals sousing out our travelling campfire
and superhighway calisthenics.

It's astonishing to imagine this is still a world at war
when we could easily barrage borders to be massive
relay team contenders.

Who will it be? Who will emerge our hero?
Surely a great one will usher in the final fire,
but it is up to all of us to protect the flame.

Flag-Bearer
for Clara Hughes

You've carried flags before – heavy,
large, white, red, black, depending on your mood,
the colour of the bender you might be on,
whether you've succumbed to surrender or were forced to fight.
You know night intimately and its secrets, how girls
fall prey to promises fluttering in the wind, how partying
without purpose can go stale as childhood dreams,
and how often sheets are used for burying.
That's when you wrapped yours around
you, sped ahead of the others – not to escape,
but to re-enter the game, plunge into a new era of sweat, blood,
and tears – not unlike the past in that sense, but this time
suffering offered meaning, pain calculation, triumph scores.
You wiped your brow with your parade of flags, embraced them
in bed, and one day woke and realized it was your own fire
kept you warm, and let them go.

Tonight, an entire country on your shoulders,
you've never felt so light.

Opening Ceremonies
(27 lines for 27 days of Olympic and Paralympic Games)

Opening hours
Opening lines
Opening up
Opening wine
Opening umbrella
Opening jokes
Opening doors
Opening oysters
Opening gifts
Opening the third eye
Opening weekend
Opening dark portal
Opening other people's mail
Opening mouth
Opening statement
Opening bid
Opening books
Opening act
Opening chakras
Opening flowers
Opening minds
Opening valves
Opening borders
Opening arms
Opening night
Opening toast
Opening soon

Open air
Open office
Open source
Open cork
Open table
Open adoption
Open access
Open kitchen
Open house
Open sesame
Open jam
Open ground
Open ended
Open concept
Open diary
Open directory
Open casting
Open circuit
Open-faced sandwiches
Open field
Open marriage
Open road
Open season
Open mic
Open bar
Open heart
Open happiness

A Brother Has Your Back
for Alexandre and Frederic Bilodeau

Remember early morning fights over Tonka trucks
and television dibs? You were only allowed to lose
to me. The rest of the world – well, they'd have to break
the doors down and set fires to get anywhere past
our chain of defence. Then fights shifted,
from schoolyard and backyard to the field
of dreams – *I can't do it, I don't think I'm*
the one, but a brother knows better, twists
those thoughts into knots, packs them into boxes,
and mails them off to detractors, *to be opened*
later, when we've proved you wrong. We have
each other's backs, and who knows those
backs best than brothers? I'm yours when
you want to back out, back down, back into,
back away, and back off. I'm your backside,
and your sidekick, your up and down, and
whichever of us climbs the hills of life
or chases possibility's fastest times, we know
the only reason either of us gets to the top
is for a better view of that most loved face
awaiting earned glory at the bottom.

Podium Haiku

Gold

Market prices, go
ahead and fluctuate, we
invest in courage.

Silver

Pure metallurgic
anniversary. Sterling
winter memories.

Bronze

I always wanted
my profile etched in metal
in my nation's mind.

Ode to 4th Place

4 elements
4 humours
4 corners of the world
4 on the floor
4 score and 7 years ago
4/4 time
4 ages of man
4 on 4 pickup
4 directions
4 gospels
4 crop rotation
4 unities
4 day workweek
4 under par
4 dimensions
4 wheeler
4 in hand knot
4 letter words
4 fold root of reason
4 food groups
4 musketeers (see: sequel)
4 cylinder engine
4 move checkmate
4 post bed
4 virtues
4 molars
4 cheese blend
4 stomachs (see: cows)
4 noble truths
4 suits of cards
Henry IV
4th Dynasty
4 Christmases
4 and 20 blackbirds
4 border state

4 seasons
4 tops
4 leaf clover
4 horsemen
4 chambers of the heart
4 the love of it

Winter Sport Abecedarian

Amazing bodies congregate:
daredevils emancipating future
glory, hearts intensely juggling
kamikaze leanings, miraculous
notions of perfection, quasi-
religious superstitions towards
ultimate velocity, weathered
x-rays yielding zen.

Ode to Sliding Sports
in memory of Nodar Kumaritashvili

*(a poem to celebrate those who dedicate their lives to
luge, skeleton, and bobsleigh)*

because every kid smiles to see a giant slide
because the body can become train
because to lose one's head is an amazing experience
because takeoff is everything
because grips are tentative
because the subtle shift of a shoulder can change solar systems
because life is slippery, enjoy when wet
because lie can be verb, noun, adjective, adverb, and preposition
because brakes are for when the ride is finished
because I've always loved the smell of floors
because I'm zooming through the ribs of a whale
because faster is faster
because pants were made for tearing
because a thousandth of a second is a lifetime
because my middle name is velocity
because my angels play whistles and cowbells
because the wind is a coach
because I can see my feet
because I can't see my feet
because riskiness is an occupational hazard
because tunnels are paths to the gods
because my future is measured in nanoseconds
because you must trust each twist and turn of your muscles
because I stuck my tongue once on a metal pole and had to
                              be inventive
because to slide or not to slide is the only question
because you can go right after me, thank you
because ice does not apologize
because my body is an icicle

because up here hangs potential
because down there I can go back up
because down is the direction of daring

If My Lover Were a Snowboarder

We'd have much more inventive names
for our positions, our cries of delight.

Tell me your imagination
doesn't hit the roof
or settle into your basement
or back door with a little more
ardour & style when presented with:

Honey, why don't we pour a little wine,
play some Barry White
& tail wheelie tonight.

Put the kids to bed early & let's get
nollie under the covers.

Don some aristocratic costumes
& caballerial...

Or

Break out the twister board & practice
rodeo flips.

You look so beautiful when you Pop Tart.

You drive me crazy when you wet cat.

Please, before we turn off
the TV & the lights
for the night, show me
your lip tricks &
I'll show you mine.

Skiing Love Poem

Mountain, I know you
choose favourites.
I seek not forgiveness,
but fervour.

In our sport, we do not fall
in love.

We set our arrows
to your whims.
Please blow
kisses on my back.

Ski Cross Love Poem

Wait for me, darling,
at the bottom of the hill,
like buried treasure.

Aerials

We dreamed of this, under the stars, camping out
in the middle of winter. Tents zipped tight, fires aglow,
snow in our boots and on our cheeks, sliding across rivers,
fishing with sticks. In the cold, the body gets ideas.

And there is always someone on a campsite
waiting to point out the hunters and bulls, big and little
dippers, scorpions and cupids, making history with light
or the milky way weaving its white banner back

to the city, even under the deepest fog. No one is alone
here with the shooting wishes and circling astronauts.
Even the snow and ice have secret names and missions,
bundle up tight before cascading down the mountain

side. All fireworks are partly human, partly magic.
Look up: fallen angels toss baskets of confetti
into our eyes, taunting us to pike, tuck, rotate.
Splashing us all with wondersky.

Cross-Country

When the moment comes
you no longer feel your
legs, or the sun, or the lips of
your boots, try not to panic –
the self still exists though in airy,
collapsible form like the perfect
party invitation, and you move
without will or energy or pull or
perhaps even consciousness
(although how would I know
at this point since I'm telling you
I'm a slip of paper in the wind);
the hills and trails, mountains
and snow coalesce around
you, happy in complacency
and chameleon colours attuned
to your white mood. Soon the tracks
will leap up and break you out of this
careless condition – the sprint is on –
dashing you to the destination address
where friends will be waving hello
as you break the seal of goodbye.

Super G Haiku

From wind & snow &
outrageous guts, I sew my own
hero costume.

Curler Want Ad

I'm looking for a man.
Actually, I'm looking for four:

Must know how to slide in slow motion,
hit and roll with the punches, rise in seconds from a kneeling
to standing position, play the nose slide, and be handy
with hammers and brooms.

Must be commitment driven and future oriented.
A planner and strategizer. Must be able to eye distances,
think fast on your feet. Must be willing to stand guard.

Will forgive lateness, as long as you hurry,
or hurry hard. Put your best foot forward.
Try not to bang heads or be distracted by
Norwegian clown pants.
Should own black gloves.
Could be bald so long as you have mojo.

Absolutely must not be afraid to walk on thin ice,
or push your weight around.

To become my vice-skip, press the button.

If we decide to go our separate ways,
I promise no fights splitting the house.
It's all part of the bonspiel of life.

But let's do our best
to sweep all the sad bits under the rug
and make love from end to end to end of the earth.

Team Pursuit

Classic story:

boy meets girl
boy loses girl
girl chases other girl
that girl goes mad
for boy next door.

Round upon round
like counting grades
until graduation.

Those of us who did not marry
our high school sweethearts
know, it's not about
nabbing the girl
but having the best time.

Bobsleigh Love Poem

Two by two chasing
adventure – you drive, I'll
figure out the brakes.

If I Could Trade Bodies

If I could trade bodies with the athlete
of my choice, I couldn't wait to squeeze myself
into a speed skater's suit, just to walk
to the corner store to buy milk or light bulbs.
I'd wear my slick new skin to make deposits
at the bank, post my packages, down
bright blue cocktails at my local. I'd even wear
my superhero garb to teach at the university –
one arm resting gallantly behind my back,
the other swinging as I explain the subtle
differences between metonymy and
synecdoche, why free verse flourishes
in America and formalism in the UK.
And if their eyes started to roll or heads
nod, I'd say, *Follow me!* and we'd take long
strong strides across campus, a massive
knowledge relay linking history and space –
facts, theories, equations, interpretations
collecting like lactic acid in my massive
thighs. I'd even embrace cut tendons
and stitches, ankle injuries and a few sordid
spills into padded walls if only to feel
wind on my back of my own making,
if only to welcome time's brave curves
with each active cell of my being.

Helmet

I tell you I am a warrior,
    not some protective shell
you wear because
    you can't really trust
yourself or your fellow ice-
    cutters to stay upright.

Treat me with care (my straps
    get sore). Don't mock, toss,
or kick me to the mouldy cellars
    of gym bags to suffocate
underneath mounds of smelly
    socks, jocks, and elbow pads.

Shine me. Notice my pressure
    against your skin, your wet hair,
the back of your neck. I too dream
    the greater glory of an arena
where I test my mettle against
    every post and board.

Figure Skates Love Poem

Foot corset, you get leaner
the longer I tug.

But once we
tie the knot, you show me,
at every opportunity,
your sharp little teeth.

Canada Hockey Poem

Mon pays,
ce n'est pas un pays,
c'est une patinoire!

Every 60 Seconds

St. Peter's Gate, but in
reverse – busting out
of paradise, an activated
diorama of sin. Even clouds
cover their eyes as you flaunt
your immodesty. Each red
flag ripe for the taking, you
swerve a serpent's track.
No kingdom, only man
& woman & a white tablet
on which to propose
new commandments.

Capturing Momentum: A Paradox

Do I hover here for the opportunity
to freeze a foot, land a limb, sandbox speed?

Momentum multiplies, motors.
To stop stasis, stalemate, suicide.

Your existence necessitates
dropping me in the dust while
I tailgate your tailwind, eulogize
your erosions.

I would like to think language
travels at the speed of light
or at the very least at the speed
of a high kick or triple jump.

But this too: paradox.

Language lassoes.
Every page a penalty lap
of punishment.

If you can't feel me
moving through you,
you certainly can't
see me.

Revising the von Trapp Score

Personally, if I had penned the famous film,
              I would have spent more time on the slopes
        than singing, more effort

on moguls than math   instead of different ages
        the siblings   on the same   national team
staggering

                                        start times
governess a coach   preparing a proper
        diet
              urging each   to a personal best.

                Growing up, other kids
got giddy at the size
                              of the mansion, I thought

              tear it
              down

                                        enjoy
                                        the view.

Each winter   those images   return as I

        catch stray tunes along

the reeling mountainside,

        ski snow pole
                    snow turn
                                    jump ski snow

turn

the hills finally   alive   with the sound

of music.

Speed Skating Love Poem

We are very pleased
to inform you the size of
the blade does matter.

Swedaly

The school children are inventing
nations &, as a sidebar, family names,
an arena its own excuse to lose
& locate new loyalties.

In Swedaly, I'm told, faces
are half-blue half-green
with white eyes, red noses,
& yellow eyebrows. Babies
are born South-Korean.
Mothers knit red Czech
sweaters for churches &
everyone comes together once a year
in Canada for a chili cook-off.

Liars! some kids call
three rows down. *Who are you?*

We're from Swedaly, they proudly
reply. *Who are you?*

This shuts them up for a time.
Not long.

Are you cheering for Italy or Sweden?

The new citizens aren't choosing.
True immigrant kids – no matter
what the score, they're keeping
their options open.

My Father as Olympian

He doesn't always feel like getting up,
but like most athletes he does, at dawn,
prepping muscles and planning the exercises
of his day down to the minute.

Meditating, he manoeuvres his life through
a mind run of potential hazards,
the twists and turns and leaps and jumps
he might face, brute opponents to ward off.

To train, he lifts his weight and more,
punch bags despair, drop-kicks his worst
memories. *Life is an obstacle course,*
he assures me. *Find your way out.*

When he worries his back may break,
again, he imagines his two children
without a father and rewinds the tape,
suits up, grabs a bite, begins to roll.

An orderly may put him to bed
each night and adjust the lights, but
my father dreams his own dreams
and runs with them.

Luge Haiku

Because physics should
not be theoretical,
I experiment.

Alternate Sport Definitions

Aerials: my body a wishbone

Penalty box: the nation's confessional

Moguls: mountain acne

Slob Air: couch surfing on snow

Shoots clean: 5 ways of looking at a blackbird

Ski Cross: cryptic crossword race

McEgg: scrambled human on buttered toast

Corner guards: ice Mounties

Hurry hard: hiding evidence of the party as Dad pulls up in the driveway

Snowboarding Results End Philosophical Debate

The half-pipe, is, without a doubt, half-full.

The Gang

Schoolyard ringleader:
pick your posse – 4 strong mates
you can count on in a pinch, who will
sign up for the full program, defend
home turf, do the dirty deeds
that need to be done.

Push, push, push –
on the margins, on the edge
of civil society, this is your mantra,
your anthem, your badge of honour.
Push, push, push, push –
now tuck, trust the team, go
along for the ride.

Navigate, negotiate the labyrinth –
cross your fingers the minotaur will reward grit,
dedication & friendship, make you master
of the maze.

Taking turns at breakneck speed –
the finish line flashes your secret handshake.

Confessions of a Biathlete

Because I like freaking out
airport security with my carry-ons – one long luggage
bag and one black secret agent suitcase.

I transport death weapons,
but the most dangerous articles exist in my mind.

there   *there*   *there*
        there   *there*

You see, life holds no surprises.
As humans, we hit things to test our ability to hit.

No need to be
ashamed of such desires:
rain and eagles and meteors aspire to similar aims.

When I was seven, I grew peculiar wings
but had yet to pick my prey.

Canada Is the Hockey Ward: Men's Version
(with nods to Ron MacLean)

Crosby your fingers.
Every Sea, brook, and mountain cheers
Go Canada Go!
Turn up the Heatley:
We need to be Thorntons in their sides.

We Boyle with excitement.
Our boys will Perry in every corner,
Make our opponents look Doughty,
Marleau their stats.
Staal Switzerland, Nash Norway,
Pronger the United States
With a Fleury of shots.
We'll get out of this what we put Iginla.

For 8 years we've been dreaming,
And Bergeron.
Like King Richards
My kingdom for a gold medal.
He who gives, Toews.
Keith the faith.

We Neidermeyer top prize.
Bragging rights must remain here,
No crossing Brodeurs.

8 years is too Luongo.
Weber or not it's destiny,
We force fate.
May the Morrow ring gold.

Canada, bow to the hockey gods.
Whoever Getzlaf laughs longest.

Canada Is the Hockey Ward: Women's Version
(with nods to Ron MacLean)

Tune up the Pipers,
Pray, if you must, to St. Pierre.
It's time to test our Kellar instinct
And Bury kings.

With every drop of the puck,
We must Poulin our resources
And fly like Agosta wind
Skating Apps and Apps around our opponents
Sending them into Sostorics.

Our women are Bonhommes
With Johnstons the size of hockey sticks.
Tough Szabados, cool customers.

We Labonte this more than anyone.
This is our Vaillancourt.
So, put your hands into your Ouellette and make the bet
For Ir-win.
It's our Botterill to climb.

And we know they'll give it 110% Hefford.
Turn it up. Get your game face on.
Enjoy the view, wash it all down with a cool Mikkelson
Or better yet a Wickenheyser.
Come on Canada, cheer as MacLeod as you can!

Human Nature

My parents say jump.
I do not jump.
My teachers say jump.
I do not jump.
My priest says jump.
I do not jump.
My boss says jump.
I do not jump.
My doctor says jump.
I do not jump.
My country says jump.
I do not jump.
My heart says jump.
I obey.

Snowboarder at the Door

Trick or treat?
Trick, trick!
Trick, trick!
Trick, trick!

Long Distance
for Brian and Robin McKeever

For us, long distance isn't lonely.
On the contrary: a long conversation in code between friends –
tin cans clasped to strings, walkie-talkie
cabin conspiracies, voice messages suspended
in humidity. I tie my skis to yours,
and climb hills at your back. You, in turn,
are always glancing behind, setting pace,
detailing the scenery.

Yours is the first draft,
mine the manuscript.
Yours the text,
mine the underlining.

It's funny how many love letters we've
abandoned in the snow. We never sign them –
can't wait to start afresh.

Who are you?
Oh yes, you are my substance and
my shadow.

You are the sun
and the sun's messenger.

The Ice Dance Is Perfect

Imagine your body
never complained of
pressure: cracks,
breaks, pain.

Your legs are your
childhood – feel them,
but only for what they will
become: your arms protect your
family – no matter how far-flung,
knowledge of home
circles the ice.

Your back, my darling,
your back, surrender to it –
like the dream lover you
never dared approach
in the light, or like that God
you once believed in who
now reaches for you.

Spell for a Hat Trick

Do it once.
Do it twice. Oh, why not,
Do it once more.

On the Low
(a sledge hockey poem)

On the low: ice
is scalpel, highway, mirror.
Like covert, contrarian spies
we pursue a circular mystery
stymied in black. Distress,
dislocation, contusion, concussion:
mere equipment adjustments.
Exiles, borders trespassed
equals freedom. We utter
blades, our fiercest desires
find solace trapped
in butterfly nets.

Judges' Tower

from the judges' tower
the heavens are knowable
& spectators snowflakes
dissolving on ground

each minute a new constellation
spars with the sun king
& jester clouds
for amusement & analysis

could be higher
could be grander
could be faster
could be spectacular

the celestial factory
pumps out product after product
measurements noted, balances
adjusted, variants approved

one day a perfect 10
will be awarded &
the judges' tower will disappear
in a puff of perfect snow

Struck by Lightning

I watch you wipe out, spectacularly –
human pinwheel manhandled by wind –
& can't conceive what your consciousness
communicates during the apex of accident
(where *is* your body in space?).

I suppose we, smugly, like to speculate
we sense disaster approaching, as if on tiptoes,
waving banners & dropping innuendoes
into conversation, & we'll adjust, activate
plan A, B, or G into immediate effect.

Yet, most often I've been shocked into
sorrow – as if struck by lightning –
spread-eagled or foetus-shaped on the sidewalk
or carpet, transfixed by the incomprehensibility
of nature, electricity, halted destiny – staring
numbly at the sadness as if it might recognize
me, strap me to a stretcher & lift me home.

You are either fearless or the ultimate realist
to propel yourself into positions of *nowhere*
(hurtling through your destiny or your agency
at the speed of...) – accepting equal probabilities
of transcendence & obliteration.

Ski Jumping Haiku

Because I once asked
my science teacher if you
could make the sun laugh.

Sledge Hockey Haiku

From this angle, ice
is infinite horizon,
eternal sunrise.

Evolution of Speed Skating

Human windmills
propagating efficient energy,
investigating new varieties
of life. Oval orbits, inside
and outside, changing
the earth's shape.

Biathlon Brings Me Closer to Religious Awakening

I now know for sure:
gods are hungry for bullets.
Martyr syndrome,
you'll acquiesce.
But I'll protest:
No, fed by bullets
heads grow larger,
messages linger.

If you cannot locate
me, to the millimetre,
then you must make up
lost time, confront
the futility of fate.

Only the gods
would invent a sport
where breath,
controlled,
commands life.

Skeleton Love Poem

The time alone has been good for me.
I've had the chance to contemplate
the nature of life and death
and the velocity of thought.

Here are my conclusions:
Worlds collapse by a twitch of a muscle.
Emotions are curved.
The end is faster than the beginning.

My Guardian Angel

Perhaps your guardian angel
sports wings, mine sprouted ski poles
& I hear her swooshing in front,
behind, above, about, below,
the surreptitious slope.

Sometimes she instructs me
in clear, crisp commands;
sometimes admonishes me
with a tough vocal hand;
sometimes applauds
as we attack brutish hills;
sometimes casts nets
if we take a nasty spill.

Our trust, to work,
must snowball.

I wax away thoughts of glory
or defeat, answering only
to your voice's flurry.

Against All Odds

I'm tight.
I can't flex my feet.
My arm broke.
My right shoulder dislocated.
My rifle jammed.
I dropped my ski pole.
My sledge cracked.
The sun got in my eyes.
My wax let me down.
My soul exploded.
My angel took a vacation.
My heart sped up.
My heart slowed down.
My heart stopped.
I smacked the gate.
I ate snow.
I tripped out of bounds.
The ref made a bad call.
God laughed at my plans.
Debris on the ice.
Rain slicked the hill.
My blood-pressure pill registered as a banned substance.
My alarm clock didn't go off.
My tendon snapped.
My guts spilled.
The training facilities shut down.
The ice made faces at me.
The devil sucked my ribs for breakfast.
My father wanted a violinist.
My mother wanted peace of mind.
My suit shrunk in the wash.
My bladder misbehaved.
I'm on a first-name basis with the operator of the helicopter.
Fate flew in the understudies.
The bank manager owns my first-born.
Ants carried off the finish line.

Hand Games

I've got a coin in my hand.
I've got a button in my hand.
I've got a toothpick in my hand.
I've got bubblegum in my hand.

I've got a message in my hand.
I've got an omen in my hand.
I've got fire in my hand.
I've got desire in my hand.

I've got a river in my hand.
I've got an eagle in my hand.
I've got mountains in my hand.
I've got an avalanche in my hand.

I've got a wedding in my hand.
I've got a baby in my hand.
I've got a century in my hand.
I've got death in my hand.

I've got nothing in my hand.
I've got something in my hand.
I've got something in my hand.
I've got nothing in my hand.

High Kick Haiku

Some gods admire our
unorthodox technique – long
legs tickling the stars.

Snow Snake Haiku

Forgive me, bear, cruel
conditions necessitate
underhandedness.

The Internal Dialogue of the Sledge Jumper

What is over the next mountain?
Another mountain?

What is over the next mountain?
Another mountain.

What is over the next mountain?
Another – mountain.

What is over the next mountain?
Another mountain!

What is over the next mountain?
Another: mountain.

What is over the next mountain?
(Another...mountain.)

What is over the next mountain?
Another mountain.

What is over the next mountain?
ANOTHER MOUNTAIN!

What is over the next mountain?
An...oth...er...mo...un...ta...in.

What is over the next mountain?
An Other mountain.

I Wish My Pets Were Athletes

After witnessing the wonders
of mushing, I think it proper & suitable,
potentially even admirable, to devise
a training program for my pets.

Feel free to follow suit
as soon as designs are drawn.

Once dressed in the colours
of our kitchen & patio set,
we will devote the hours
we used to spend watching
TV, doing tricks for treats
or strolling about the block
without earning medals or
eternal glory, to a perfectly
timed schedule, measured diet,
inspirational meditation.

I know this will bring
human & beast together –
we both desire greatness,
we both like to stretch
& to jump with joy.

What a wonder it would be
to proudly hoist my pets upon a podium.

What an honour to sing sonorously
as our night blanket is raised on our roof.

Team Canada Hockey Love Poem

Each nation rises
to its anthem –
ours composed
daily on ice.

In Praise of Zamboni Drivers

& all other eyes & ears, arms & legs
behind the mountains & trees
clearing snow or trucking it in
flooding ice, setting courses
parking cars & scheduling buses
flipping burgers & brewing coffee
gatekeeping, judging, tabulating
inputting, weighing, escorting
translating, pouring, organizing
selling jerseys & toques
& muffins & mugs & mittens
forgiving yet rarely forgiven
scurrying about tracks and slopes
you too deserve a poem before spectators
dash to washrooms or hotdogs
or to check text messages, console
a loved one, just a few seconds where
we all stop fretting & fussing & cheering
& daydreaming & look around
give a gentle nod to all those eyes, ears,
arms, legs we've barely noted hovering there
all those forest creatures busily
about their business before
the oncoming racket chases them away

Aerials Haiku

Winter awakens,
clouds flip, birds scissor, the sky
performs jumping jacks.

Lament for Disqualification

As if the planet itself has ceased
to exist, your mind deleted,
your body blacklisted. The power
of rules & trespassing consequences
all too clear – like Moses denied
the promised land, Adam & Eve
paradise, Ovid his house of love.
We bow our heads with yours –
can't believe our eyes. We beg the gods
to intervene, hit replay, revise
the story's end.

But the chapter has been written,
shame photo taken, the *Why? Why? Why?*
press conference with no good answers
on their way.

Thousands of unrecognized errors will occur
tonight between these walls alone – lament those
alongside the poor sot caught putting just
one foot over the line.

Curling Love Poem

Against all sound love
advice, I remain a stone.
You sweep around me.

Sleepless Nights
for the parents

Layer upon layer of warm clothing, banners of hope –
one more long flight & endless drive, one more sleepless night,
one more rounding up of half-asleep siblings & homegrown signs,
coffee & cowbells, one more slathering of red & white paint.

Now, stuck in line; pressed against the gate; now time to wait.

No matter what, you know you will be proud.
Nevertheless, you also understand the fickleness of winter –
its strange sense of humour – raging temperaments
of water & wind, the callousness of cold.

Now it's time: your child drops out of the sky
riding rivers & clouds. Miraculous bundle.
Snow your seasonal surrogate.

Advice from a Speed Skater

Stay low to the ground.
When there's an opening, pass on the inside.
Beware of those who get close so
they can trip you up.
Be your own machine.
Be your own speed demon.
A second skin is essential,
not necessarily a thick skin.
Everything that's ever happened
will happen again & probably
within seconds.
Trust time – you don't
have the luxury of watching the clock.
When needed, give your
friends a strong push.

At the end of life,
stick your foot out.
Better yet, kick.

We Dream in the Language of Winter

20 different words for snow
45 different words for pain
1 word for win

Luge Love Poem

I luge you.
I luge you not.
I luge you.

Ice Opera
for Joannie Rochette

No one had to say, *Get out on that ice.*
Nobody needed to give you a nudge.
You were born to spin and spiral,
serve the gods of spectacle and suspense.
You courted the music in your heart,
soared with it, sharpening your edges,
softening landings.

If the stands were nearly empty, you imagined
crowds, you the heroine in an ice opera,
roses flung at your feet, the roar
of encores, the scores of symphonies.

But tonight, while we listen to the orchestra and
thunder applause, you are skating to a new
sanctum of silence, of shadows and silhouettes,
where mother and daughter mouth the words
to all the secret love songs ever written.

Closing Ceremonies
(27 lines for 27 days of Olympic and Paralympic Games)

Closing prayers
Closing ranks
Closing circle
Closing remarks
Closing sale
Closing costs
Closing stock
Closing lanes
Closing bell
Closing entries
Closing iris
Closing signature
Closing accounts
Closing argument
Closing knit stitch
Closing jump rings
Closing wounds
Closing business
Closing network connections
Closing paragraph
Closing hot tub
Closing hand on puck
Closing questions
Closing frontier
Closing dimensions
Closing day
Closing credits

Close loop
Close deal
Close the gap
Closed captioning
Close lids
Close tabs
Close parliament
Close call
Close vents
Close laptop
Close bar fridge
Close browser
Close interval
Close quotes
Close journal
Close fireplace
Close palms
Close cottage
Close windows
Close button
Closed deck
Close combat
Close highway
Close encounter
Close eyes
Close down
Closed 'til next season

Numerology

25.69 4:04.84   26.75   2   1   43.241   1:16.56
52.36   1:57.14   221.57   1   6:55.73   332.28   333.13
4:09.137   2-0   202.64   6-7   40.981   46.366   6:44.224
1   1   3:24.85   6-3   3-2

=

silver bronze   gold   silver   gold   silver   gold
gold   silver   gold   gold   bronze   gold   silver
silver   gold   bronze   silver   gold   bronze   gold
gold   gold   bronze   gold   gold

Other People's Dreams

For months now I have donned skis
& skin-tight suits, launched myself into
sleighs & sleds & across ice surfaces.
I am a woman of many flags – nations
argue over citizenship – but all I care
about is speed & lift & height & landing
clean. My world is reduced now
to manageable illusions. Thank you
for the privilege & novelty. I recognize
fellow athletes by a narrow all-consuming
focus & a sense of humour for anything
to do with wind. I drown, I fly, I shed
teeth & skin & other things that happen
routinely in dreams – the stuff of
psychiatric careers. But I know these
specific dreams, on the pinnacle of
success, on the teetering balance of
my ankles & talent & the curve of
the track, your thoughts & songs
& sweet nothings opined to lovers
are not exactly mine. Still, I'm happy
to go along for the ride. I'm happy,
for once, to insist on nothing but
what is possible.

Play Like a Paralympian

When the sailboat my father was on capsized in the Caribbean, he was a changed man. The contaminated water he swallowed caused his quadriplegia. His life was radically transformed from a successful immigrant story to a tale of tragedy.

At the time of his accident, in the 1970s, he was essentially told his life was over. He retired from his job. My mother left him. He didn't even qualify for single-parent benefits because the government had not accounted for a single *man* caregiver – the benefits were strictly "single mother."

But my father has always been a determined, stubborn, and passionate man, and these traits ballooned after his accident. All his energy was now focused on ensuring his children would succeed and find stability in the world. Like many South Asian parents, he emphasized our intellectual talents, telling me often, *Your brain will get you out.* But he also encouraged us to play sports, I think because he didn't want us to take our bodies for granted. My father had loved swimming and tennis.

I will confess that I was skeptical about whether Canadians would embrace hosting the 2010 Paralympic Games. Most people don't know much about the Paralympics. This is problem number one. Many confuse the Paralympics with the Special Olympics, which it isn't. Paralympians are elite athletes with world rankings in their disciplines. Special Olympians have mental disabilities and the focus of their games is on participation, which is valuable, but different from the focus of the Paralympics, which is athletic excellence. Problem number two is that people tend to assume that watching disabled athletes will be depressing – remind them of their own fragility and mortality. Problem number three is that many people have little contact with people with disabilities and this inexperience only perpetuates stereotypes of what the disabled are able to accomplish.

In actuality, Paralympic athletics is invigorating, an awe-inspiring representation of human spirit and will mixed with human ingenuity. And the Paralympic athletes were welcomed by a sold-out crowd at BC Place with cheering and dancing. Video montages of Terry Fox's journey across Canada and Rick Hansen's Man in Motion world tour reminded us that two of Canada's most famous athletes of all time are disabled, and their inspiration is still felt internationally today.

But logistically, how do you play hockey without ice skates? What does it feel like to sit-ski? How does a blind biathlete shoot targets? How do you aim stones in wheelchair curling? Viewing the sports in person or on television certainly helped answer these practical questions. In addition, each competition venue featured a "Play Like a Paralympian" station where the public could try out Paralympic sports equipment and learn in a hands-on manner what skills disabled athletes develop to succeed in a given discipline. Both adults and children were encouraged to participate in these interactive spaces, and line-ups to try out sledges and sit-skis and wheelchair curling were steady throughout the day.

At Whistler, I sat in a mono-ski, the type of ski used by most alpine athletes in the "sitting" categories (those who have injuries or disabilities affecting their lower bodies). Sitting skiers are sometimes faster than able-bodied Olympians because their weight is closer to the ground, therefore acute turning skills are required to negotiate downhill and slalom gates, and one must control the ski as it acts as a spring on bumps, propelling the athlete through the air. Arm and core strength are essential to balance the mono-ski and keep the skier from toppling over. *When you see a skier fall,* the volunteer told me, *you know what strength it takes for the athlete to push the ski back up and continue down the hill.* I couldn't hold myself upright, nor could I even get out of the mono-ski by myself. Thankfully, no one wanted to send me down the slopes blind-folded to teach me about visually impaired alpine skiing.

Sledge hockey equipment for each player is typically a sledge (custom-designed lightweight titanium sleds with long skate blades attached underneath and straps to bind the players to the seats) and two short hockey sticks, one for each hand, with metal picks on top, which the players reverse and put to the ice to move forwards and backwards along the ice rink. The equipment available for test-driving by spectators was adjusted to a "floor hockey" version – sledges on wheels instead of blades, and short hockey sticks without the picks for playing on non-ice surfaces. Hockey is hockey, and Canadians won't give up the chance to play hockey whenever the opportunity arises, so the space dedicated to instructing would-be sledge hockey players (able-bodied or not) was the most popular at each venue. Volunteers set up mini sledge races and two-minute matches for the children. Again, arm strength is key to propel yourself down the ice. And since sledge hockey teams have fewer players than stand-up hockey (what sledge hockey players call conventional hockey), you are propelling yourself down the ice a lot. This is why sledge hockey periods are fifteen minutes rather than twenty.

Other equipment available for testing included a laser rifle used by visually impaired biathletes, a cross-country sit-ski (without the springing action of most alpine sit-skis), and the long sticks, like fire pokers with hooks, used to slide stones across the ice in wheelchair curling. Wheelchair curling is even more technical for the stone thrower than conventional curling because there are no sweepers to help navigate the stones.

The "Play Like a Paralympian" stations confirmed to me that familiarity and exposure builds interest and excitement for any sport. Children jumped into the equipment. Adults were fascinated by the technological developments required to stage the sports. I enjoyed learning the rules of the games and the skills the athletes must develop to excel. One just needs the opportunity for involvement. Which is why it was disappointing that very little coverage of the games was available on television or in newspapers. For Paralympic sport to grow its fan base, coverage to create familiarity of the sports and the athletes is crucial.

Each Paralympic sport, although based on conventional able-bodied sport categories, is in many ways an entirely new sport, or at least another distinct version of the game. If sport were a language – and it might be – we could call these versions dialects. Last fall, gold medallist sledge hockey player Billy Bridges told me about a film called *Sledhead*, by David McIlvride, a documentary following Billy and a handful of other players through their journey to the World Championships, that was showing during a Toronto film festival highlighting representations of disability. My partner Chris and I attended the screening. And we were forced to revise what we thought we knew about hockey. Yes, the rules for scoring in sledge hockey and stand-up hockey are the same. And most of the rules regarding penalties, offsides, icing, and faceoffs are also the same. But, as already outlined, these athletes play strapped into sledges and move about the rink by utilizing two short hockey sticks with shooting blades on one end and picks on the other.

So what does that mean for the game, besides utilizing a different mode of transport on the rink? It means that when they hit each other against the boards, they are hitting each other *with their entire bodies* and they are hitting each other on the part of the boards where there is *zero give*. The picks are violent weapons that the players are not shy to use on each other when they get into a scuffle or when they are fighting for the puck along the boards. At one point in the film, a player lifts his jersey so the camera can capture the multitude of jabs suffered during the game – his entire torso littered with bleeding or scabbing puncture holes. It also means, if you're a goalie, almost every shot is aimed *at your face*. Goalie Paul Rosen claims Billy has knocked out at least a dozen of his teeth, just in practice. And I know that Billy's fiancée, two-time Olympic gold medallist and one-time silver medallist women's hockey goalie Sami Jo Small, has found that aspect of the sport a little hard to get used to as she sometimes straps on the sled and her goalie mask for the Ontario guys if they can't train with their team goalies. These men are a lot tougher than most

NHL players. And they want to win just as badly. For many, the game is their life, their entry into a life, away from being "physically challenged" persons, to persons who physically challenge themselves.

I took a friend to the slalom events who would not normally have considered attending the Paralympic Games. Yet, within minutes of watching the start of the competition, she asked me if it was possible that the Paralympics were more fascinating than the Olympics. In many ways, yes. In fact, I know several sports advocates who are convinced that those involved with the Olympics (not the athletes, but the bureaucrats and business people) are afraid of the Paralympics. The Paralympics offer compelling stories of unique personalities overcoming adversity. The ways in which each participant utilizes personal training and technology to compensate for physical limitations cultivates diverse approaches to each sport, not to mention engineering breakthroughs. The success of the underdog is a fundamental human narrative, one that breeds passion in athletes and spectators alike. The weaknesses of the athletes are on the surface, and figuring out how the athlete will need to strategize according to particular weaknesses is part of the pleasure and intrigue of the games. *I can't believe a person can do that,* is a frequently expressed comment, something you don't always hear in conventional sport.

The visually impaired biathletes, for instance, shoot with rifles that emit electronic audio signals that indicate when they are aiming at the target. Guns are adjusted, in advance, to each athlete's specifications. The most extreme innovation in the rifle portion of the race was without a doubt that of German Paralympic legend Josef Giesen. He is missing both arms – skiing the course on the power of his legs alone. And he fires his rifle with his teeth. Yes, *with his teeth!* And he usually shoots clean.

The logistics are not just important for the success of the athlete, but are essential to ensure as much safety as possible. In winter sport, after all, falls and spills and dangerous speeds are par for the course for fully sighted and able-bodied athletes. In visually impaired skiing, the courage (or reckless-ness, depending on your point of view) to ski, let alone race, without the ability to see the course is part of the appeal of this sport category. Spectators can't quite believe what they are seeing. When races are delayed due to low visibility, this is done mostly for the sake of the guides. Guides are also, by necessity, elite athletes themselves. Most have skied compet-itively at a national if not international level and have been recruited as guides if they've fallen just short of qualifying times, if they've recently retired, or if personal reasons lead them in this direction. Robin McKeever decided to dedicate his skiing career to guiding his brother Brian – and they are among the most decorated Paralympic athletes in history. Brian qualified for the 2010 Olympics, and so Robin must also maintain Olympic shape to stay in front of his brother.

The guides are involved in the competition as much as the athletes themselves – although, again, try to put yourself in the visually impaired athlete's shoes or skis and imagine what it must be like to rely nearly exclusively on the vocal commands of your guide to instruct your body to get through a challenging and dangerous course in the quickest time pos-sible. How it works: guides can ski in front or behind (although most ski in front); guides can be either gender; guides com-municate with their athletes by radio microphone. In cross-country races, you can actually see and hear the guide talking, calling to, and encouraging the athlete. Guides are also con-tinually glancing behind to ensure their athletes are not too close or too far – again, a real challenge in downhill where the speeds are blistering and spills can be life-threatening. If the athlete is too close, a collision can occur. I saw one race where the guide fell and the athlete could not go on alone, although technically, only the athlete is required to cross the finish line.

In winter Paralympics, medals are awarded to both ath-letes and guides. For a reason that no one has been able to explain to me yet, guides do not receive medals for summer Paralympics. The acknowledgement of training, dedication, and accomplishment that a medal offers is a motivating factor for guides. Summer Paralympics guide medals would encourage more elite athletes to perform this crucial role in a visually impaired athlete's life. It would also help to build important relationships inside and outside of sport.

For some, Paralympics is an uplifting celebration of the human spirit, but to me it's also the flicking of a giant middle-finger up to fate, a fuck-you to anyone who ever said you shouldn't or couldn't. These athletes not only deal with the massive challenges of competitive sport that all elite athletes face, but they must also live with illness, injury, and the prejudices attached to them. Some of the competing athletes were born with their disabilities, some were able-bodied athletes who suffered accidents, some are victims of violence or war veterans (in fact, the Paralympics have their origins in athletic competitions organized by Dr. Ludwig Guttmann for British wounded in World War ii). They each have discovered strategies and coping mechanisms to use pain as an intense, motivating force, and not to get bogged down in the "Why me?" question. They just admit pain, rather than fight it: *Yes, I'm in pain. Yes, this is really hard. So what? That doesn't mean I'm going to stop.* Which is a fundamental narrative of most sport, and the basis of our fascination with it.

The Arctic Games Experience

The first time I heard of the Arctic Winter Games was from my friend Ann Peel, who had attended the games in her capacity as executive director of the charity Right to Play. She raved about the events, particularly the aboriginal arctic sports such as the One-Foot High Kick or Arm Pull, as well as the differences in competitive culture displayed here, where athletes offer each other advice throughout the process and the audience, for the most part, is expected to be silent. *My boys were young and I was worried they were going to cause trouble, that they wouldn't keep quiet, especially after taking them to the Olympics,* Ann told me, *but they were mesmerized by the athletes' quickness, dexterity, balance, and stillness. They told me they liked the Arctic Games the best, Paralympics second, and Olympics third.*

Commissioner James Smith (Yukon), Commissioner Stuart Hodgson (Northwest Territories), and Governor Walter Hickel (Alaska), began the Arctic Winter Games in 1969. The impetus behind the movement was to encourage quality competition among northern athletes who were otherwise isolated, and therefore facilitate development of physical and mental skills as well as cultural exchange. The first Arctic Winter Games was held in Yellowknife, Northwest Territories, in 1970 with contingents from Yukon, Northwest Territories, and Alaska. Northern Alberta sent its first contingent in 1986. In 1988 invitations were also extended to Greenland, Northern Quebec, and Russia.

In 1988 it was also decided that the cultural events and Arctic Sports would be given more prominence and importance in the games, and that Dene Games, another aboriginal collection of sports, would be added to the programming. In 1996 organizers agreed to shift the primary focus of the games to youth. By 2000, adults were only included in the cultural events, Arctic Sports, and Dene Games. The Sami people from Northern Scandinavia and participants from Yamal, Russia, also joined the roster. (The rule for inclusion is that territories must lie above the 55th parallel.) And women and junior girls, traditionally barred from various Arctic Sports and Dene Games, were now given clearance to compete.

For the 2010 Arctic Winter Games, held in Grande Prairie, Alberta, I was especially curious to observe the aboriginal sports and cultural events, though it's worth noting that most of the sports programming reflects more common global summer and winter Olympic sports categories, such as basketball, volleyball, wrestling, gymnastics, hockey, indoor soccer, and figure skating; furthermore, the majority of the participating body of youth are non-aboriginal. For many who live in the participating regions, this is the only major competition available to youth athletes and part of the concept behind the games is to encourage more interaction and dialogue among diverse geographical populations and particularly among aboriginals and other ethnic groups.

The nine teams that participated in these games were Alaska, Alberta North, Greenland, Northwest Territories, Nunavik (Quebec), Nunavut, Sápmi (Scandinavia), Yamal-Nenets (Russia), and Yukon. Participants were as young as eleven in some sports (such as dog-mushing, which includes juvenile and junior categories) and as old as in their thirties for the Dene Games (which includes junior and adult categories). The motto for the games was "Dream, achieve, inspire." The aboriginal sports, divided into Arctic Sports and Dene Games categories, were as follows:

Arctic Sports: Open Male: One-Foot High Kick; Two-Foot High Kick; Alaskan High Kick; Kneel Jump; Airplane; One Hand Reach; Head Pull; Knuckle Hop; Sledge Jump; Triple Jump; All Around (all events).

Open Female, Junior Male, and Junior Female: One-Foot High Kick; Two-Foot High Kick; Alaskan High Kick; Kneel Jump;

Arm Pull; Sledge Jump; Triple Jump; All Around (best three individual events).

Competitors must enter a minimum of four events in the Open Female, Junior Female and Junior Male categories and a minimum of seven events in the Open Male category.

Dene Games: Open Male, Junior Male, Junior Female, and Juvenile Female: Finger Pull; Hand Games (team); Snow Snake; Stick Pull; Pole Push (team); All Around (total score of the three individual events).

Not knowing what to expect from this list of unfamiliar sport activities, I was grateful to have a guide with me, Greg Edgelow, the director of the Yukon Aboriginal Sport Circle, a man with a wicked sense of humour and a lot of patience, who explained that all the aboriginal sports have a basis in survival techniques, either mimicking hunting or other life skills or survival actions, or building skills of strength and balance for use in future life situations. Most are short, repetitive actions, with calculations based on height, distance, or elimination of an opponent. A distinction frequently made between the Dene Games and the Arctic Sports is that the Dene Games are more strategic and privilege slyness, cunning, quick thinking, and strength (both mental and physical), whereas the Arctic Games are more athletic and acrobatic.

My first Dene Games event brought me inside an indoor tent shaking with intense monotonous drumming, where teams began bouncing, screeching, flailing, gesticulating wildly, shaking and punching and closing and opening hands. This was Hand Games, Greg explained, a form of traditional gambling (their version of poker), but very physical as the players taunt, mock, hex, and dance as they try to psych out their opponents and embody the rhythm of the game, which is understood to be much like the rhythms of nature (some experience the flow of a river, others the personae of animals – for hand gestures, several mimic horns or antlers).

The drums are meant to speed the game up and also allow participants a rare form of self-expression, especially for the normally subdued personality, and almost every team has at least one player that seems possessed by the music, the game, and greater spirits. Reactions to wrong guesses by their opponents might be aptly described as "dissing." And yet, the game is extremely friendly, as team members smile, pat each other on the back, and shake hands after particularly good rounds. The announcer claimed that men used to bet their wives in Hand Games. Some believe the chances are fifty-fifty no matter what, but those people are not players of the game. Those who play believe it is a game of skill, deceit, trickery, and power dynamics. The teammates are selected for their skill in the other Dene Games events but all must still learn and participate in Hand Games.

Next, we headed over to the gymnasium for the Two-Foot High Kick. Players can start from a running or standing approach, but the fur target (called a seal), dangling from an apparatus usually well above their heads, must be struck with both feet parallel. Upon landing, both feet must hit the floor at the same time, no more than shoulder-width apart, and the player must maintain balance and control. The junior girls winner hit six feet two inches, and the adult males winner eight feet.

One-Foot High Kick and Alaskan High Kick are variations on the same theme. In the One-Foot High Kick, the competitor kicks the seal with the foot he/she must land upon. In the Alaskan High Kick, competitors are seated on the floor and must hold one foot with an opposite hand, lift and kick the seal with the other foot, maintaining balance on the one-foot landing, still holding the other foot off the ground. Competitors are allowed three attempts at the given height. If successful, the seal is raised four inches for men and two inches for women. The heights achieved are beyond the heights of the competitors in all the categories, but the scores are highest for the One-Foot High Kick, next for the Two-Foot High Kick, and then the Alaskan High Kick. These kicks were useful to hunters and whalers to signal that prey had been acquired or to point out live prey to others without having to yell (which might not be heard anyway, or might alert one's prey) and without hard-to-see hand gestures. Whether a one-foot or two-foot kick would be employed would be based on the specific landscape, weather, the distance between the kicker and those to be signalled, and the type of signal the kick was meant to convey. The Alaskan High Kick seems to be more of a training exercise in building coordination, balance, and strength.

The following day was the Sledge Jump competition. Much like hurdles, the athletes hit, crash, and break sledges; however, unlike hurdles, sledges are built like shorter versions of gymnastic vaults (approx. two feet high and wide and six feet in length), covered by a blanket or fur. The competitor must jump over ten sledges lined in a row, pausing for no more than five seconds before heading back. Competitors must jump with both feet together, land with both feet together, and not hit the sledge. The sport is based on the practice by reindeer herders of jumping over their sleds. Sledge Jump, I discovered, is for the hardcore. In other words, primarily for Russians. The Russian men can literally jump hundreds of sledges before tiring out or tapping one for disqualification (the record is 830). Although all other categories offer three attempts, the open male category, due to the Russian contingent, is given only a single attempt. One of the coaches told me that this is because otherwise the event can run until one or two o'clock in the morning. Officials sometimes have to beg the Russians to stop, if they're not going to attempt to break the world record. I saw a Russian jump 390 sledges, while other athletes – remember these are athletes – could not scale more than a handful. I watched, riveted, all day.

For Kneel Jump, competitors begin on their knees, feet behind them. They can swing their arms, but cannot rock their legs, and then must propel themselves forward, landing on two feet and holding their landing. Scoring is determined by distance. This sport is derived from a survival skill needed for ice fishing. As most would fish on their knees on ice floes, if a floe began to break away, or ice crack, the fisherman would need to jump quickly – in a single action – to a safer spot.

Arm Pull and Stick Pull are person versus person competitions. Arm Pull is much like arm wrestling, except here the competitors are on the floor and lock their legs. They pull each other's arms by hooking elbows. In Stick Pull, competitors each grab an end of a birch or spruce stick (the stick resembles a drumstick, twelve inches long, two inches in diameter) lathered in Crisco, and must pull the stick to their end, either forcing the opponent to let go or keeping the stick to one's side for at least ten seconds. These sports are intended to build pulling strength, crucial for pulling sleighs, supplies, furs, and animals. Stick Pull mimics the act of gripping large, slippery fish out of the water. In earlier competitions, bear fat or blubber was used instead of Crisco.

Snow Snake, much like javelin, is a hunting sport. However, in Snow Snake the throw is underhanded and the spear is thrown down an icy track. Scoring is measured by distance. This sport mimics the act of killing sleeping prey. The technique of throwing the spear along the ice, rather than up in the air, would increase the chances of success over long distances and extreme windy weather.

Rather than displaying the going-into-war, battle-until-death attitude of many conventional sports competitions, athletes displayed a sense of humour during the events, laughing at themselves, at fate, at the event itself, at life. The Russian men who had dominated Sledge Jump could not hit the seal even once in the Alaskan High Kick. They laughed. Other competitors tried to help, even well after the event was over. *Next time, next time you will hit it.* Players encouraged each other, regardless of team designation, gave each other tips, and applauded each other's outcomes. It was sometimes hard to determine the winner, as the athletes did not shout, or pound fists, or gloat, or run around with flags on their backs. They smiled, shook hands, and moved on to the next event. At one point the audience was invited to try an exhibition Alaskan sport: the Butt Hop. You sit on the ground and cross your legs together in front of you. They must never touch the ground as you try to hop on your bum to the finish line. I couldn't hop even once. I have no idea what survival skill I'm lacking, but I'm definitely lacking it. The Arctic Games do not just encourage humility among the participants, but among audience members too.

The cultural programming was equally diverse and impressive, as each competing team brings along an artistic contingent. These artists performed daily at venues around the city over the lunch hour, at gala events, and inside the athlete village. Artists were encouraged to meet and learn from each other's practice, thereby mimicking the athletic experience. Artist mentorship programs were also instituted to encourage youth art-making, the results of which were displayed in galleries alongside the professional art. There was even an "Art of the Spectator" component: art supplies distributed at various sports venues with spectators invited to offer their own unique interpretation of the games. The cultural programming was a crucial component of the overall sport experience, intersecting with the athletes, the spectators, and encouraging exchanges and understanding between cultures. A pavilion dedicated to pin-trading – a common hobby of the athletes – was erected for people to meet each other, tell the stories behind their pins (where they acquired them, from whom, what year the pins were made, in which country), and swap for new pins. And the aboriginal sports events culminated with a banquet dinner and dance for all the athletes, coaches, and artists.

For someone who has lived in Canada and graduated through its school systems my entire life, and who has a PhD with a specialization in Canadian literature, I am surprised and embarrassed to say that this was my first encounter with aboriginal sport. Canadian history and cultural studies, not to mention physical education, curricula ought to consider exposing youth to these sports, native to Canada before the advent of hockey and lacrosse. I firmly believe there is a sport for everyone. Expanding winter sports definitions in our communities is a way of building cultural appreciation and understanding, and opening up new possibilities for the body, mind, and heart.

Acknowledgements

Thank you, Diana Kuprel at *The Literary Review of Canada* for offering me "Poet's Corner" for my daily journalistic dispatches and poems. Thank you to Helen Walsh, Naoko Asano, Alastair Cheung, plus others for working on the site. Thank you to Meagan Walton for keeping on track with the daily poems posted on canadianathletcsnow.ca and to Leigh Nash for updating priscilauppal.ca.

Thank you, CBC, especially Matt Galloway, for your unfailing support for my ventures, and for taking a chance that listeners were eager to hear sport poems. Thank you as well to Mary Ito, and other hosts, both national and regional, for featuring poems.

Thanks to the editors/producers at *Vancouver Sun,* Shaw Radio and TV, *Frogpond,* and *Exile: The Literary Quarterly* for featuring poems.

Thank you, Sonnet L'Abbé, for the much-needed place to crash and the company.

Thanks, SSHRC and York University Faculty of Arts Small Research Grants, for much-appreciated funding, as well as all the participants in Bodyworks Symposium, especially my co-organizer Dr. Suzanne Zelazo, and Ann Peel and Dr. Bruce Kidd, all as eager as I am to bring together the sports and arts worlds. Thank you, Greg Edgelow at the Yukon Aboriginal Sports Circle, for your time and expert insight at the Arctic Games in Grande Prairie, Alberta.

Thank you, York University and all members of the Creative Writing Program and English Department, especially Rishma Dunlop, Julia Creet, Tom Loebel, Art Redding, and Rose Crawford, for your support. Thank you to my graduate assistants, especially Dennis Hill, for helping with prep work.

Thank you, everyone at the Canadian Athletes Now Fund, but especially visionary founder and executive director Jane Roos, the always enthusiastic Conrad Leinemann, and the sometimes silent but wicked Meagan Walton. I'd like to encourage anyone who has ever felt inspired by watching our athletes perform to donate to the fund. The money goes directly to the athletes to help offset nutrition, coaching, and equipment costs. Nearly 80 percent of the Olympic athletes competing in Vancouver were supported by the fund. All Paralympic athletes who applied were also supported by the fund. Approximately 90 percent of the athletes who will likely be competing in 2012 at the London Olympics and Paralympics will have been supported through the fund.

Thanks, Alexandra Orlando, Ann Peel, Sami Jo Small, Justin Connidis and Julia MacArthur, Annamay Pierce, Ben Rutledge, Jake Weizal, Jennifer Botterill, Kevin Light, Pat Bolger, June Roos, the Wootherspoon family, and many more, for making the Athlete House such a vibrant place to be.

Thank you, Barney Bentall, Great Big Sea, and God Made Me Funky, for those phenomenal private concerts. And thank you, Jeremy Roenick, for concluding, "You're really deep, aren't you?"

Thank you, Billy Bridges, Dean Penny, Jit and Jen Uppal, Emmitt Uppal, Richard Teleky, Barry Callaghan, David Layton, Meaghan Strimas, Tim Hanna and Tracy Carbert, Charles Boyes and Dani Spinosa, Leigh Nash and Andrew Faulkner, for offering support and encouragement.

Thank you, Denis De Klerck, Stuart Ross, and everyone at Mansfield Press, for believing in this project.

Thank you to my other supportive sport-art enthusiast friends, especially my fellow Canadian poets and fiction writers who don skates and running shoes and the maple leaf without apology.

Thank you, most of all, to all the Canadian athletes for your inspiration, passion, and boundless energy, and for your open and generous response to poetry! Thank you as well to your family and friends who lit up the CANFund Athlete House with their love.

Love to Christopher Doda, for joining me for Valentine's Day, as well as for cheering during all my workouts, literary and otherwise.

Priscila Uppal is a Toronto poet, fiction writer, and York University professor. Among her publications are seven collections of poetry, most recently *Ontological Necessities* (2006; shortlisted for the $50,000 Griffin Poetry Prize), *Traumatology* (2010), and *Successful Tragedies: Poems 1998-2010* (Bloodaxe Books, U.K.); and the critically acclaimed novels *The Divine Economy of Salvation* (2002) and *To Whom It May Concern* (2009). Her work has been published internationally and translated into numerous languages. For more information visit priscilauppal.ca.

BOOKS FROM MANSFIELD PRESS

POETRY
Leanne Averbach, *Fever*
Diana Fitzgerald Bryden, *Learning Russian*
Alice Burdick, *Flutter*
Margaret Christakos, *wipe.under.a.love*
Pino Coluccio, *First Comes Love*
Gary Michael Dault, *The Milk of Birds*
Pier Giorgio Di Cicco, *Early Works*
Christopher Doda, *Aesthetics Lesson*
Rishma Dunlop, *Metropolis*
Suzanne Hancock, *Another Name for Bridge*
Jason Heroux, *Emergency Hallelujah*
Carole Glasser Langille, *Late in a Slow Time*
Jeanette Lynes, *The Aging Cheerleader's Alphabet*
David W. McFadden, *Be Calm, Honey*
Leigh Nash, *Goodbye, Ukulele*
Lillian Nećakov, *The Bone Broker*
Peter Norman, *At the Gates of the Theme Park*
Natasha Nuhanovic, *Stray Dog Embassy*
Catherine Owen & Joe Rosenblatt, with Karen Moe, *Dog*
Corrado Paina, *Souls in Plain Clothes*
Jim Smith, *Back Off, Assassin! New & Selected Poems*
Robert Earl Stewart, *Something Burned Along the Southern Border*
Steve Venright, *Floors of Enduring Beauty*
Brian Wickers, *Stations of the Lost*

FICTION
Marianne Apostolides, *The Lucky Child*
Kent Nussey, *A Love Supreme*
Tom Walmsley, *Dog Eat Rat*

NON-FICTION
Pier Giorgio Di Cicco, *Municipal Mind*
Amy Lavender Harris, *Imagining Toronto*